The Statutory Requirements

Year 1 and Year 2

To purchase a copy please visit:

www.TheNationalCurriculum.com

or scan this code to take you there:

© Crown copyright 2014

Corporate Author: The Department For Education

Published by: Shurville Publishing

This document is available for download at www.gov.uk/government/publications

ISBN: 978-0-9930644-6-3

Contents

Year 1   4

1.0 English
1.1 Spoken Word   5
1.2 Word Reading   5
1.3 Comprehension   6
1.4 Writing – Transcription   7
1.5 Writing – Handwriting   8
1.6 Writing – Composition   8
1.7 Writing – Grammar, Vocabulary and Punctuation   8

2.0 Maths
2.1 Number – Number and Place Value   10
2.2 Number – Addition and Subtraction   10
2.3 Number – Multiplication and Division   10
2.4 Number – Fractions   11
2.5 Measurement   11
2.6 Geometry – Properties of Shape   12
2.7 Geometry – Position and Direction   12

3.0 Science
3.1 Working Scientifically   13
3.2 Plants   13
3.3 Animals, inc. Humans   13
3.4 Everyday Materials   14
3.5 Seasonal Changes   14

4.0 Non-Core Subjects
4.1 Art & Design   15
4.2 Computing   15
4.3 Design & Technology   16
4.4 Geography   17
4.5 History   18
4.6 Music   18
4.7 PE   19

Year 2   20

1.0 English
1.1 Spoken Word   21
1.2 Word Reading   21
1.3 Comprehension   22
1.4 Writing – Transcription   23
1.5 Writing – Handwriting   24
1.6 Writing – Composition   24

1.7 Writing – Grammar, Vocabulary and Punctuation   25

2.0 Maths

2.1 Number – Number and Place Value   26
2.2 Number – Addition and Subtraction   26
2.3 Number – Multiplication and Division   27
2.4 Number – Fractions   27
2.5 Measurement   27
2.6 Geometry – Properties of Shape   28
2.7 Geometry – Position and Direction   28
2.8 Statistics   29

3.0 Science

3.1 Working Scientifically   30
3.2 Living Things and Their Habitats   30
3.3 Plants   31
3.4 Animals, inc. Humans   31
3.5 Use of Everyday Materials   31

4.0 Non-Core Subjects

4.1 Art & Design   32
4.2 Computing   32
4.3 Design & Technology   33
4.4 Geography   34
4.5 History   35
4.6 Music   35
4.7 PE   36

Year 1

1.1 Spoken Word

Pupils should be taught to:

- Listen and respond appropriately to adults and their peers ask relevant questions to extend their understanding and knowledge
- Use relevant strategies to build their vocabulary
- Articulate and justify answers, arguments and opinions
- Give well-structured descriptions, explanations and narratives for different purposes, including for expressing feelings
- Maintain attention and participate actively in collaborative conversations, staying on topic and initiating and responding to comments
- Use spoken language to develop understanding through speculating, hypothesising, imagining and exploring ideas
- Speak audibly and fluently with an increasing command of Standard English
- Participate in discussions, presentations, performances, role play, improvisations and debates
- Gain, maintain and monitor the interest of the listener(s)
- Consider and evaluate different viewpoints, attending to and building on the contributions of others
- Select and use appropriate registers for effective communication.

1.2 Word Reading

Pupils should be taught to:

- Apply phonic knowledge and skills as the route to decode words
- Respond speedily with the correct sound to graphemes (letters or groups of letters) for all 40+ phonemes, including, where applicable, alternative sounds for graphemes

- Read accurately by blending sounds in unfamiliar words containing gpcs that have been taught

- Read common exception words, noting unusual correspondences between spelling and sound and where these occur in the word

- Read words containing taught gpcs and –s, –es, –ing, –ed, –er and –est endings

- Read other words of more than one syllable that contain taught gpcs

- Read words with contractions [for example, i'm, i'll, we'll], and understand that the apostrophe represents the omitted letter(s)

- Read aloud accurately books that are consistent with their developing phonic knowledge and that do not require them to use other strategies to work out words

- Re-read these books to build up their fluency and confidence in word reading.

1.3 Comprehension

Pupils should be taught to:

- Develop pleasure in reading, motivation to read, vocabulary and understanding by:
- Listening to and discussing a wide range of poems, stories and non-fiction at a level beyond that at which they can read independently
- Being encouraged to link what they read or hear read to their own experiences
- Becoming very familiar with key stories, fairy stories and traditional tales, retelling them and considering their particular characteristics
- Recognising and joining in with predictable phrases
- Learning to appreciate rhymes and poems, and to recite some by heart
- Discussing word meanings, linking new meanings to those already known
- Understand both the books they can already read accurately and fluently and those they listen to by:
- Drawing on what they already know or on background information and vocabulary provided by the teacher
- Checking that the text makes sense to them as they read and correcting inaccurate reading

- Discussing the significance of the title and events
- Making inferences on the basis of what is being said and done
- Predicting what might happen on the basis of what has been read so far
- Participate in discussion about what is read to them, taking turns and listening to what others say
- Explain clearly their understanding of what is read to them.

1.4 Writing – Transcription

Spelling (see English Appendix 1, available online)

Pupils should be taught to:

Spell:

- Words containing each of the 40+ phonemes already taught
- Common exception words
- The days of the week
- Name the letters of the alphabet:
- Naming the letters of the alphabet in order
- Using letter names to distinguish between alternative spellings of the same sound
- Add prefixes and suffixes:
- Using the spelling rule for adding –s or –es as the plural marker for nouns and the third person singular marker for verbs
- Using the prefix un–
- Using –ing, –ed, –er and –est where no change is needed in the spelling of root words [for example, helping, helped, helper, eating, quicker, quickest]
- Apply simple spelling rules and guidance, as listed in English Appendix 1
- Write from memory simple sentences dictated by the teacher that include words using the gpcs and common exception words taught so far.

1.5 Writing – Handwriting

Pupils should be taught to:

- sit correctly at a table, holding a pencil comfortably and correctly
- Begin to form lower-case letters in the correct direction, starting and finishing in the right place
- Form capital letters
- Form digits 0-9
- Understand which letters belong to which handwriting 'families' (i.e. Letters that are formed in similar ways) and to practise these.

1.6 Writing – Composition

Pupils should be taught to:

Write sentences by:

- Saying out loud what they are going to write about
- Composing a sentence orally before writing it
- Sequencing sentences to form short narratives
- Re-reading what they have written to check that it makes sense
- Discuss what they have written with the teacher or other pupils
- Read aloud their writing clearly enough to be heard by their peers and the teacher.

1.7 Writing – Grammar, Vocabulary and Punctuation

Pupils should be taught to:

- Develop their understanding of the concepts set out in English Appendix 2 by:
- Leaving spaces between words
- Joining words and joining clauses using and

- Beginning to punctuate sentences using a capital letter and a full stop, question mark or exclamation mark

- Using a capital letter for names of people, places, the days of the week, and the personal pronoun 'I'

- Learning the grammar for year 1 in English Appendix 2

- Use the grammatical terminology in English Appendix 2 in discussing their writing.

2.1 Number – Number and Place Value

Pupils should be taught to:

- Count to and across 100, forwards and backwards, beginning with 0 or 1, or from any given number
- Count, read and write numbers to 100 in numerals; count in multiples of twos, fives and tens
- Given a number, identify one more and one less
- Identify and represent numbers using objects and pictorial representations including the number line, and use the language of: equal to, more than, less than (fewer), most, least
- Read and write numbers from 1 to 20 in numerals and words.

2.2 Number – Addition and Subtraction

Pupils should be taught to:

- Read, write and interpret mathematical statements involving addition (+), subtraction (−) and equals (=) signs
- Represent and use number bonds and related subtraction facts within 20
- Add and subtract one-digit and two-digit numbers to 20, including zero
- Solve one-step problems that involve addition and subtraction, using concrete objects and pictorial representations, and missing number problems such as $7 = \{\} - 9$.

2.3 Number – Multiplication and Division

Pupils should be taught to:

- Solve one-step problems involving multiplication and division, by calculating the answer using concrete objects, pictorial representations and arrays with the support of the teacher.

2.4 Number – Fractions

Pupils should be taught to:

- Recognise, find and name a half as one of two equal parts of an object, shape or quantity
- Recognise, find and name a quarter as one of four equal parts of an object, shape or quantity.

2.5 Measurement

Pupils should be taught to:

- Compare, describe and solve practical problems for:
- Lengths and heights [for example, long/short, longer/shorter, tall/short, double/half]
- Mass/weight [for example, heavy/light, heavier than, lighter than]
- Capacity and volume [for example, full/empty, more than, less than, half, half full, quarter]
- Time [for example, quicker, slower, earlier, later]
- Measure and begin to record the following:
- Lengths and heights
- Mass/weight
- Capacity and volume
- Time (hours, minutes, seconds)
- Recognise and know the value of different denominations of coins and notes
- Sequence events in chronological order using language [for example, before and after, next, first, today, yesterday, tomorrow, morning, afternoon and evening]
- Recognise and use language relating to dates, including days of the week, weeks, months and years

- Tell the time to the hour and half past the hour and draw the hands on a clock face to show these times.

2.6 Geometry – Properties of Shape

Pupils should be taught to:

- Recognise and name common 2-D and 3-D shapes, including:
- 2-D shapes [for example, rectangles (including squares), circles and triangles]
- 3-D shapes [for example, cuboids (including cubes), pyramids and spheres].

2.7 Geometry – Position and Direction

Pupils should be taught to:

- Describe position, direction and movement, including whole, half, quarter and three-quarter turns.

3.1 Working Scientifically

During years 1 and 2, pupils should be taught to use the following practical scientific methods, processes and skills through the teaching of the programme of study content:

- Asking simple questions and recognising that they can be answered in different ways
- Observing closely, using simple equipment
- Performing simple tests
- Identifying and classifying
- Using their observations and ideas to suggest answers to questions
- Gathering and recording data to help in answering questions.

3.2 Plants

Pupils should be taught to:

- Identify and name a variety of common wild and garden plants, including deciduous and evergreen trees
- Identify and describe the basic structure of a variety of common flowering plants, including trees.

3.3 Animals, inc. Humans

Pupils should be taught to:

- Identify and name a variety of common animals including fish, amphibians, reptiles, birds and mammals
- Identify and name a variety of common animals that are carnivores, herbivores and omnivores

- Describe and compare the structure of a variety of common animals (fish, amphibians, reptiles, birds and mammals, including pets)
- Identify, name, draw and label the basic parts of the human body and say which part of the body is associated with each sense.

3.4 Everyday Materials

Pupils should be taught to:

- Distinguish between an object and the material from which it is made
- Identify and name a variety of everyday materials, including wood, plastic, glass, metal, water, and rock
- Describe the simple physical properties of a variety of everyday materials
- Compare and group together a variety of everyday materials on the basis of their simple physical properties.

3.5 Seasonal Changes

Pupils should be taught to:

- Observe changes across the four seasons
- Observe and describe weather associated with the seasons and how day length varies

4.1 Art & Design

Pupils should be taught:

- To use a range of materials creatively to design and make products
- To use drawing, painting and sculpture to develop and share their ideas, experiences and imagination
- To develop a wide range of art and design techniques in using colour, pattern, texture, line, shape, form and space
- About the work of a range of artists, craft makers and designers, describing the differences and similarities between different practices and disciplines, and making links to their own work.

4.2 Computing

Pupils should be taught to:

- Understand what algorithms are; how they are implemented as programs on digital devices; and that programs execute by following precise and unambiguous instructions
- Create and debug simple programs
- Use logical reasoning to predict the behaviour of simple programs
- Use technology purposefully to create, organise, store, manipulate and retrieve digital content
- Recognise common uses of information technology beyond school
- Use technology safely and respectfully, keeping personal information private; identify where to go for help and support when they have concerns about content or contact on the internet or other online technologies.

4.3 Design & Technology

Through a variety of creative and practical activities, pupils should be taught the knowledge, understanding and skills needed to engage in an iterative process of designing and making. They should work in a range of relevant contexts [for example, the home and school, gardens and playgrounds, the local community, industry and the wider environment].

When designing and making, pupils should be taught to:

Design

- Design purposeful, functional, appealing products for themselves and other users based on design criteria
- Generate, develop, model and communicate their ideas through talking, drawing, templates, mock-ups and, where appropriate, information and communication technology

Make

- Select from and use a range of tools and equipment to perform practical tasks [for example, cutting, shaping, joining and finishing]
- Select from and use a wide range of materials and components, including construction materials, textiles and ingredients, according to their characteristics

Evaluate

- Explore and evaluate a range of existing products
- Evaluate their ideas and products against design criteria
- Technical knowledge
- Build structures, exploring how they can be made stronger, stiffer and more stable
- Explore and use mechanisms [for example, levers, sliders, wheels and axles], in their products.
- Cooking & Nutrition

Pupils should be taught to:

- Use the basic principles of a healthy and varied diet to prepare dishes
- Understand where food comes from.

4.4 Geography

Pupils should be taught to:

Locational knowledge

- Name and locate the world's seven continents and five oceans
- Name, locate and identify characteristics of the four countries and capital cities of the United Kingdom and its surrounding seas

Place knowledge

- Understand geographical similarities and differences through studying the human and physical geography of a small area of the United Kingdom, and of a small area in a contrasting non-European country

Human and physical geography

- Identify seasonal and daily weather patterns in the United Kingdom and the location of hot and cold areas of the world in relation to the Equator and the North and South Poles

Use basic geographical vocabulary to refer to:

- Key physical features, including: beach, cliff, coast, forest, hill, mountain, sea, ocean, river, soil, valley, vegetation, season and weather
- Key human features, including: city, town, village, factory, farm, house, office, port, harbour and shop

Geographical skills and fieldwork

- Use world maps, atlases and globes to identify the United Kingdom and its countries, as well as the countries, continents and oceans studied at this key stage
- Use simple compass directions (North, South, East and West) and locational and

directional language [for example, near and far; left and right], to describe the location of features and routes on a map

- Use aerial photographs and plan perspectives to recognise landmarks and basic human and physical features; devise a simple map; and use and construct basic symbols in a key
- Use simple fieldwork and observational skills to study the geography of their school and its grounds and the key human and physical features of its surrounding environment.

4.5 History

Pupils should be taught about:

- Changes within living memory. Where appropriate, these should be used to reveal aspects of change in national life
- Events beyond living memory that are significant nationally or globally [for example, the Great Fire of London, the first aeroplane flight or events commemorated through festivals or anniversaries]
- The lives of significant individuals in the past who have contributed to national and international achievements. Some should be used to compare aspects of life in different periods [for example, Elizabeth I and Queen Victoria, Christopher Columbus and Neil Armstrong, William Caxton and Tim Berners-Lee, Pieter Bruegel the Elder and LS Lowry, Rosa Parks and Emily Davison, Mary Seacole and/or Florence Nightingale and Edith Cavell]
- Significant historical events, people and places in their own locality.

4.6 Music

Pupils should be taught to:

- Use their voices expressively and creatively by singing songs and speaking chants and rhymes
- Play tuned and untuned instruments musically

- Listen with concentration and understanding to a range of high-quality live and recorded music

- Experiment with, create, select and combine sounds using the inter-related dimensions of music.

4.7 PE

Pupils should be taught to:

- Master basic movements including running, jumping, throwing and catching, as well as developing balance, agility and co-ordination, and begin to apply these in a range of activities

- Participate in team games, developing simple tactics for attacking and defending

- Perform dances using simple movement patterns.

Year 2

1.1 Spoken Word

Pupils should be taught to:

- Listen and respond appropriately to adults and their peers
- Ask relevant questions to extend their understanding and knowledge
- Use relevant strategies to build their vocabulary
- Articulate and justify answers, arguments and opinions
- Give well-structured descriptions, explanations and narratives for different purposes, including for expressing feelings
- Maintain attention and participate actively in collaborative conversations, staying on topic and initiating and responding to comments
- Use spoken language to develop understanding through speculating, hypothesising, imagining and exploring ideas
- Speak audibly and fluently with an increasing command of Standard English
- Participate in discussions, presentations, performances, role play, improvisations and debates
- Gain, maintain and monitor the interest of the listener(s)
- Consider and evaluate different viewpoints, attending to and building on the contributions of others
- Select and use appropriate registers for effective communication.

1.2 Word Reading

Pupils should be taught to:

- Continue to apply phonic knowledge and skills as the route to decode words until automatic decoding has become embedded and reading is fluent
- Read accurately by blending the sounds in words that contain the graphemes taught so

far, especially recognising alternative sounds for graphemes

- Read accurately words of two or more syllables that contain the same graphemes as above
- Read words containing common suffixes
- Read further common exception words, noting unusual correspondences between spelling and sound and where these occur in the word
- Read most words quickly and accurately, without overt sounding and blending, when they have been frequently encountered
- Read aloud books closely matched to their improving phonic knowledge, sounding out unfamiliar words accurately, automatically and without undue hesitation
- Re-read these books to build up their fluency and confidence in word reading.

1.3 Comprehension

Pupils should be taught to:

- Develop pleasure in reading, motivation to read, vocabulary and understanding by:
- Listening to, discussing and expressing views about a wide range of contemporary and classic poetry, stories and non-fiction at a level beyond that at which they can read independently
- Discussing the sequence of events in books and how items of information are related
- Becoming increasingly familiar with and retelling a wider range of stories, fairy stories and traditional tales
- Being introduced to non-fiction books that are structured in different ways
- Recognising simple recurring literary language in stories and poetry
- Discussing and clarifying the meanings of words, linking new meanings to known vocabulary
- Discussing their favourite words and phrases
- Continuing to build up a repertoire of poems learnt by heart, appreciating these and reciting some, with appropriate intonation to make the meaning clear
- Understand both the books that they can already read accurately and fluently and those

that they listen to by:

- Drawing on what they already know or on background information and vocabulary provided by the teacher
- Checking that the text makes sense to them as they read and correcting inaccurate reading
- Making inferences on the basis of what is being said and done
- Answering and asking questions
- Predicting what might happen on the basis of what has been read so far
- Participate in discussion about books, poems and other works that are read to them and those that they can read for themselves, taking turns and listening to what others say
- Explain and discuss their understanding of books, poems and other material, both those that they listen to and those that they read for themselves.

1.4 Writing – Transcription

Spelling (see English Appendix 1, available online)

Pupils should be taught to:

Spell by:

- Segmenting spoken words into phonemes and representing these by graphemes, spelling many correctly
- Learning new ways of spelling phonemes for which one or more spellings are already known, and learn some words with each spelling, including a few common homophones
- Learning to spell common exception words
- Learning to spell more words with contracted forms
- Learning the possessive apostrophe (singular) [for example, the girl's book]
- Distinguishing between homophones and near-homophones
- Add suffixes to spell longer words, including –ment, –ness, –ful, –less, –ly
- Apply spelling rules and guidance, as listed in English Appendix 1
- Write from memory simple sentences dictated by the teacher that include words using

the gpcs, common exception words and punctuation taught so far.

1.5 Writing – Handwriting

Pupils should be taught to:

- Form lower-case letters of the correct size relative to one another
- Start using some of the diagonal and horizontal strokes needed to join letters and understand which letters, when adjacent to one another, are best left unjoined
- Write capital letters and digits of the correct size, orientation and relationship to one another and to lower case letters
- Use spacing between words that reflects the size of the letters.

1.6 Writing – Composition

Pupils should be taught to:

- Develop positive attitudes towards and stamina for writing by:
- Writing narratives about personal experiences and those of others (real and fictional)
- Writing about real events
- Writing poetry
- Writing for different purposes
- Consider what they are going to write before beginning by:
- Planning or saying out loud what they are going to write about
- Writing down ideas and/or key words, including new vocabulary
- Encapsulating what they want to say, sentence by sentence
- Make simple additions, revisions and corrections to their own writing by:
- Evaluating their writing with the teacher and other pupils
- Re-reading to check that their writing makes sense and that verbs to indicate time are used correctly and consistently, including verbs in the continuous form
- Proof-reading to check for errors in spelling, grammar and punctuation [for example,

ends of sentences punctuated correctly]

- Read aloud what they have written with appropriate intonation to make the meaning clear.

1.7 Writing – Grammar, Vocabulary and Punctuation

Pupils should be taught to:

- Develop their understanding of the concepts set out in English Appendix 2 by:
- Learning how to use both familiar and new punctuation correctly (see English Appendix 2), including full stops, capital letters, exclamation marks, question marks, commas for lists and apostrophes for contracted forms and the possessive (singular)
- Learn how to use:
- Sentences with different forms: statement, question, exclamation, command
- Expanded noun phrases to describe and specify [for example, the blue butterfly]
- The present and past tenses correctly and consistently including the progressive form
- Subordination (using when, if, that, or because) and co-ordination (using or, and, or but)
- The grammar for year 2 in English Appendix 2
- Some features of written Standard English
- Use and understand the grammatical terminology in English Appendix 2 in discussing their writing.

2.1 Number – Number and Place Value

Pupils should be taught to:

- Count in steps of 2, 3, and 5 from 0, and in tens from any number, forward and backward
- Recognise the place value of each digit in a two-digit number (tens, ones)
- Identify, represent and estimate numbers using different representations, including the number line
- Compare and order numbers from 0 up to 100; use <, > and = signs
- Read and write numbers to at least 100 in numerals and in words
- Use place value and number facts to solve problems.

2.2 Number – Addition and Subtraction

Pupils should be taught to:

- Solve problems with addition and subtraction:
- Using concrete objects and pictorial representations, including those involving numbers, quantities and measures
- Applying their increasing knowledge of mental and written methods
- Recall and use addition and subtraction facts to 20 fluently, and derive and use related facts up to 100
- Add and subtract numbers using concrete objects, pictorial representations, and mentally, including:
- A two-digit number and ones
- A two-digit number and tens
- Two two-digit numbers
- Adding three one-digit numbers
- Show that addition of two numbers can be done in any order (commutative) and

subtraction of one number from another cannot

- Recognise and use the inverse relationship between addition and subtraction and use this to check calculations and solve missing number problems.

2.3 Number – Multiplication and Division

Pupils should be taught to:

- Recall and use multiplication and division facts for the 2, 5 and 10 multiplication tables, including recognising odd and even numbers
- Calculate mathematical statements for multiplication and division within the multiplication tables and write them using the multiplication ($\times$), division ($\div$) and equals ($=$) signs
- Show that multiplication of two numbers can be done in any order (commutative) and division of one number by another cannot
- Solve problems involving multiplication and division, using materials, arrays, repeated addition, mental methods, and multiplication and division facts, including problems in contexts.

2.4 Number – Fractions

Pupils should be taught to:

- Recognise, find, name and write fractions of a length, shape, set of objects or quantity
- Write simple fractions and recognise the equivalence

2.5 Measurement

- Pupils should be taught to:
- Choose and use appropriate standard units to estimate and measure length/height in

any direction (m/cm); mass (kg/g); temperature (°C); capacity (litres/ml) to the nearest appropriate unit, using rulers, scales, thermometers and measuring vessels

- Compare and order lengths, mass, volume/capacity and record the results using >, < and =

- Recognise and use symbols for pounds (£) and pence (p); combine amounts to make a particular value

- Find different combinations of coins that equal the same amounts of money

- Solve simple problems in a practical context involving addition and subtraction of money of the same unit, including giving change

- Compare and sequence intervals of time

- Tell and write the time to five minutes, including quarter past/to the hour and draw the hands on a clock face to show these times

- Know the number of minutes in an hour and the number of hours in a day.

2.6 Geometry – Properties of Shape

Pupils should be taught to:

- Identify and describe the properties of 2-D shapes, including the number of sides and line symmetry in a vertical line

- Identify and describe the properties of 3-D shapes, including the number of edges, vertices and faces

- Identify 2-D shapes on the surface of 3-D shapes [for example, a circle on a cylinder and a triangle on a pyramid]

- Compare and sort common 2-D and 3-D shapes and everyday objects.

2.7 Geometry – Position and Direction

Pupils should be taught to:

- Order and arrange combinations of mathematical objects in patterns and sequences

- Use mathematical vocabulary to describe position, direction and movement, including movement in a straight line and distinguishing between rotation as a turn and in terms of right angles for quarter, half and three-quarter turns (clockwise and anti-clockwise).

2.8 Statistics

Pupils should be taught to:

- Interpret and construct simple pictograms, tally charts, block diagrams and simple tables
- Ask and answer simple questions by counting the number of objects in each category and sorting the categories by quantity
- Ask and answer questions about totalling and comparing categorical data.

3.1 Working Scientifically

During years 1 and 2, pupils should be taught to use the following practical scientific methods, processes and skills through the teaching of the programme of study content:

- Asking simple questions and recognising that they can be answered in different ways
- Observing closely, using simple equipment
- Performing simple tests
- Identifying and classifying
- Using their observations and ideas to suggest answers to questions
- Gathering and recording data to help in answering questions.

3.2 Living Things and Their Habitats

Pupils should be taught to:

- Explore and compare the differences between things that are living, dead, and things that have never been alive
- Identify that most living things live in habitats to which they are suited and describe how different habitats provide for the basic needs of different kinds of animals and plants, and how they depend on each other
- Identify and name a variety of plants and animals in their habitats, including micro-habitats
- Describe how animals obtain their food from plants and other animals, using the idea of a simple food chain, and identify and name different sources of food.

3.3 Plants

Pupils should be taught to:

- Observe and describe how seeds and bulbs grow into mature plants
- Find out and describe how plants need water, light and a suitable temperature to grow and stay healthy.

3.4 Animals, inc Humans

Pupils should be taught to:

- Notice that animals, including humans, have offspring which grow into adults
- Find out about and describe the basic needs of animals, including humans, for survival (water, food and air)
- Describe the importance for humans of exercise, eating the right amounts of different types of food, and hygiene.

3.5 Use of Everyday Materials

Pupils should be taught to:

- Identify and compare the suitability of a variety of everyday materials, including wood, metal, plastic, glass, brick, rock, paper and cardboard for particular uses
- Find out how the shapes of solid objects made from some materials can be changed by squashing, bending, twisting and stretching.

4.1 Art & Design

Pupils should be taught:

- To use a range of materials creatively to design and make products
- To use drawing, painting and sculpture to develop and share their ideas, experiences and imagination
- To develop a wide range of art and design techniques in using colour, pattern, texture, line, shape, form and space
- About the work of a range of artists, craft makers and designers, describing the differences and similarities between different practices and disciplines, and making links to their own work.

4.2 Computing

Pupils should be taught to:

- Understand what algorithms are; how they are implemented as programs on digital devices; and that programs execute by following precise and unambiguous instructions
- Create and debug simple programs
- Use logical reasoning to predict the behaviour of simple programs
- Use technology purposefully to create, organise, store, manipulate and retrieve digital content
- Recognise common uses of information technology beyond school
- Use technology safely and respectfully, keeping personal information private; identify where to go for help and support when they have concerns about content or contact on the internet or other online technologies.

4.3 Design & Technology

Through a variety of creative and practical activities, pupils should be taught the knowledge, understanding and skills needed to engage in an iterative process of designing and making. They should work in a range of relevant contexts [for example, the home and school, gardens and playgrounds, the local community, industry and the wider environment].

When designing and making, pupils should be taught to:

Design

- Design purposeful, functional, appealing products for themselves and other users based on design criteria
- Generate, develop, model and communicate their ideas through talking, drawing, templates, mock-ups and, where appropriate, information and communication technology

Make

- Select from and use a range of tools and equipment to perform practical tasks [for example, cutting, shaping, joining and finishing]
- Select from and use a wide range of materials and components, including construction materials, textiles and ingredients, according to their characteristics

Evaluate

- Explore and evaluate a range of existing products
- Evaluate their ideas and products against design criteria

Technical knowledge

- Build structures, exploring how they can be made stronger, stiffer and more stable
- Explore and use mechanisms [for example, levers, sliders, wheels and axles], in their products.

Cooking & Nutrition

Pupils should be taught to:

Key stage 1

- Use the basic principles of a healthy and varied diet to prepare dishes
- Understand where food comes from.

4.4 Geography

Pupils should be taught to:

Locational knowledge

- Name and locate the world's seven continents and five oceans
- Name, locate and identify characteristics of the four countries and capital cities of the United Kingdom and its surrounding seas

Place knowledge

- Understand geographical similarities and differences through studying the human and physical geography of a small area of the United Kingdom, and of a small area in a contrasting non-European country

Human and physical geography

- Identify seasonal and daily weather patterns in the United Kingdom and the location of hot and cold areas of the world in relation to the Equator and the North and South Poles
- Use basic geographical vocabulary to refer to:
- Key physical features, including: beach, cliff, coast, forest, hill, mountain, sea, ocean, river, soil, valley, vegetation, season and weather
- Key human features, including: city, town, village, factory, farm, house, office, port, harbour and shop

Geographical skills and fieldwork

- Use world maps, atlases and globes to identify the United Kingdom and its countries, as well as the countries, continents and oceans studied at this key stage

- Use simple compass directions (North, South, East and West) and locational and directional language [for example, near and far; left and right], to describe the location of features and routes on a map
- Use aerial photographs and plan perspectives to recognise landmarks and basic human and physical features; devise a simple map; and use and construct basic symbols in a key
- Use simple fieldwork and observational skills to study the geography of their school and its grounds and the key human and physical features of its surrounding environment.

4.5 History

Pupils should be taught about:

- Changes within living memory. Where appropriate, these should be used to reveal aspects of change in national life
- Events beyond living memory that are significant nationally or globally [for example, the Great Fire of London, the first aeroplane flight or events commemorated through festivals or anniversaries]
- The lives of significant individuals in the past who have contributed to national and international achievements. Some should be used to compare aspects of life in different periods [for example, Elizabeth I and Queen Victoria, Christopher Columbus and Neil Armstrong, William Caxton and Tim Berners-Lee, Pieter Bruegel the Elder and LS Lowry, Rosa Parks and Emily Davison, Mary Seacole and/or Florence Nightingale and Edith Cavell]
- Significant historical events, people and places in their own locality.

4.6 Music

Pupils should be taught to:

- Use their voices expressively and creatively by singing songs and speaking chants and rhymes

- Play tuned and untuned instruments musically

- Listen with concentration and understanding to a range of high-quality live and recorded music

- Experiment with, create, select and combine sounds using the inter-related dimensions of music.

4.7 PE

Pupils should be taught to:

- Master basic movements including running, jumping, throwing and catching, as well as developing balance, agility and co-ordination, and begin to apply these in a range of activities

- Participate in team games, developing simple tactics for attacking and defending

- Perform dances using simple movement patterns